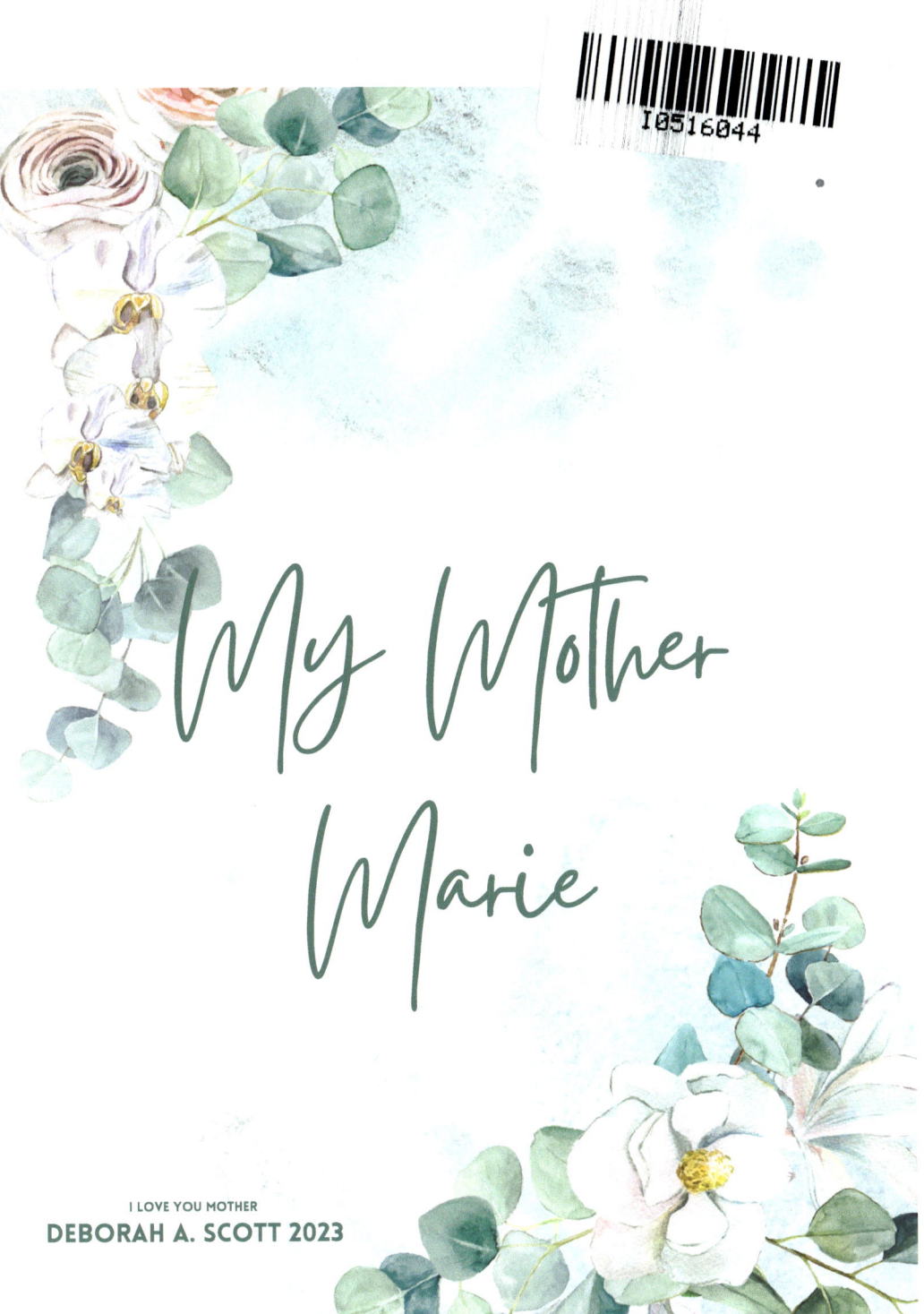

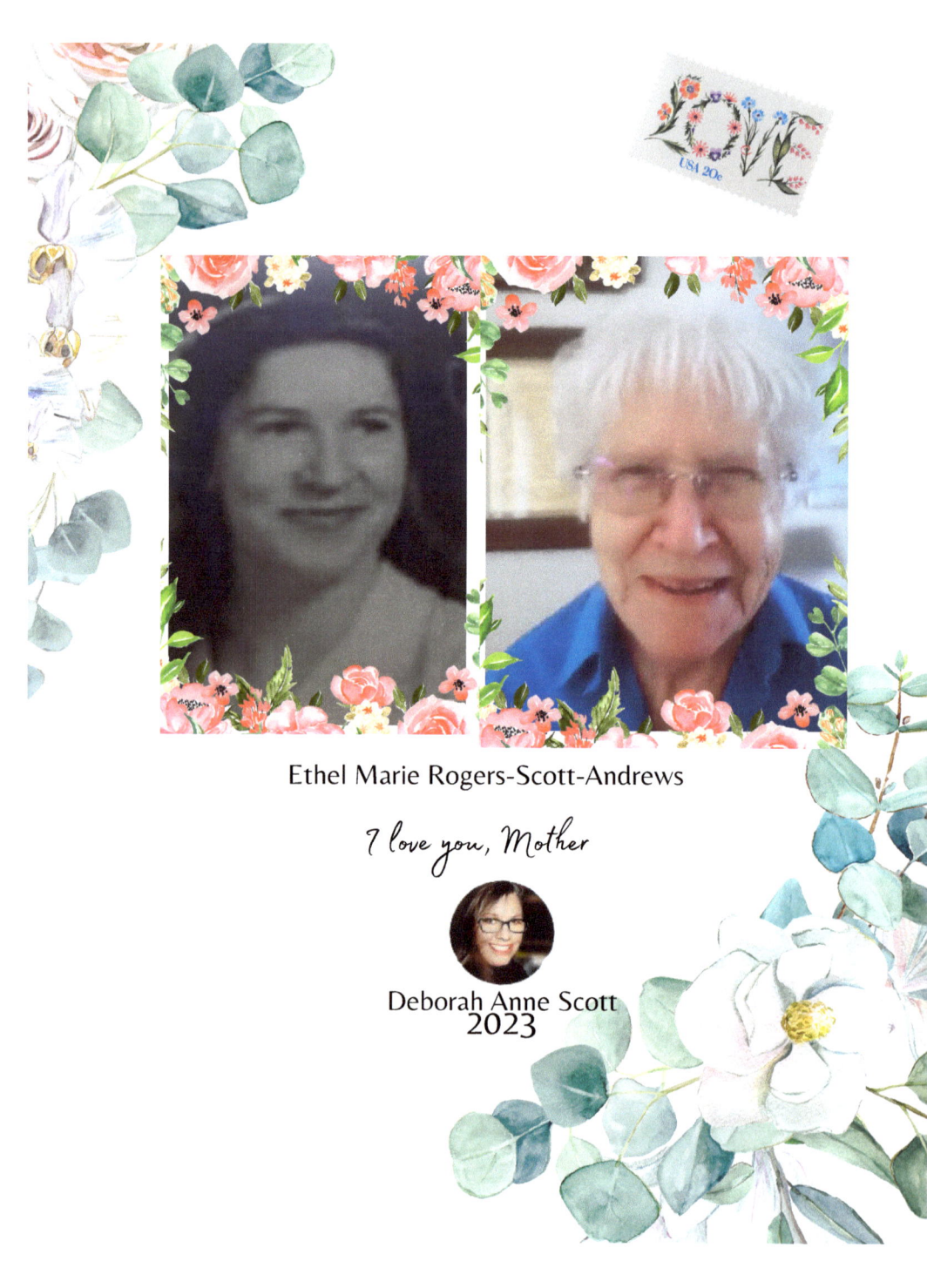

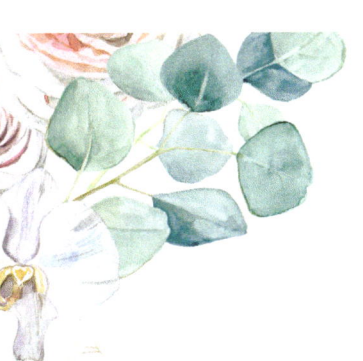

Introduction

Art is an expressive form of creativity that allows individuals to convey their emotions, experiences, and perspectives. For one woman Marie, my mother, art became a passion that helped her cope with the ups and downs of life. This manuscript tells the story of a woman who was born in 1928, raised seven children and went on to become an artist, teaching herself how to watercolor and paint with acrylics.

Her life is a testament to the power of resilience, determination, and the pursuit of one's passion.

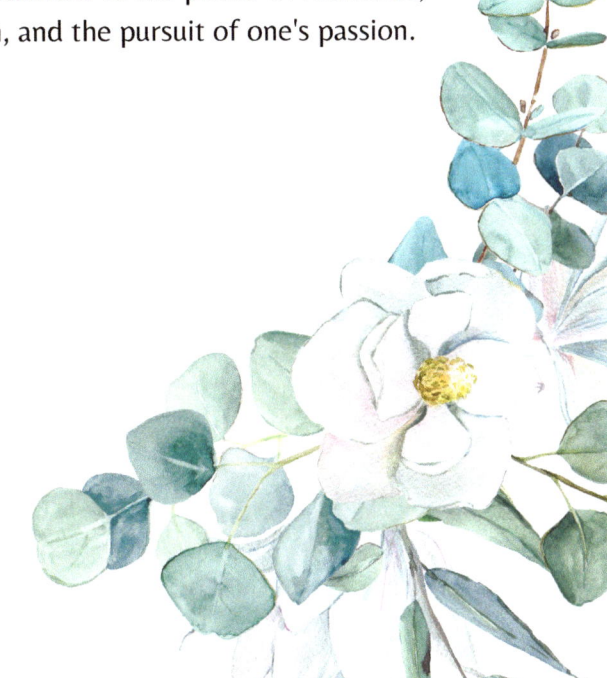

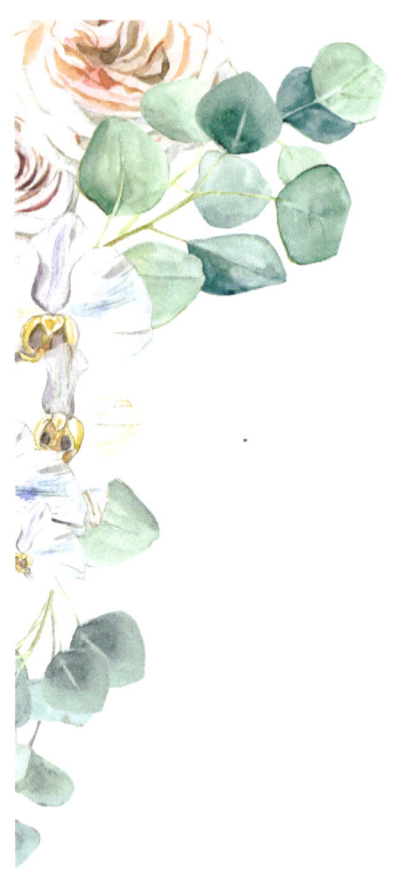
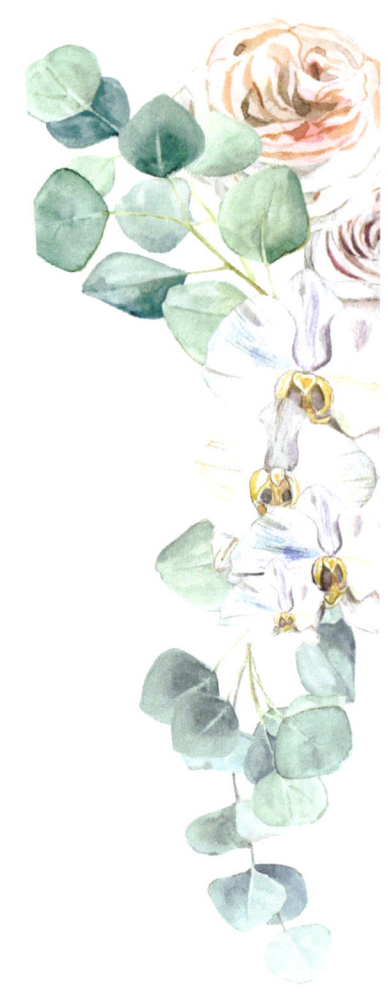

One

Beginnings

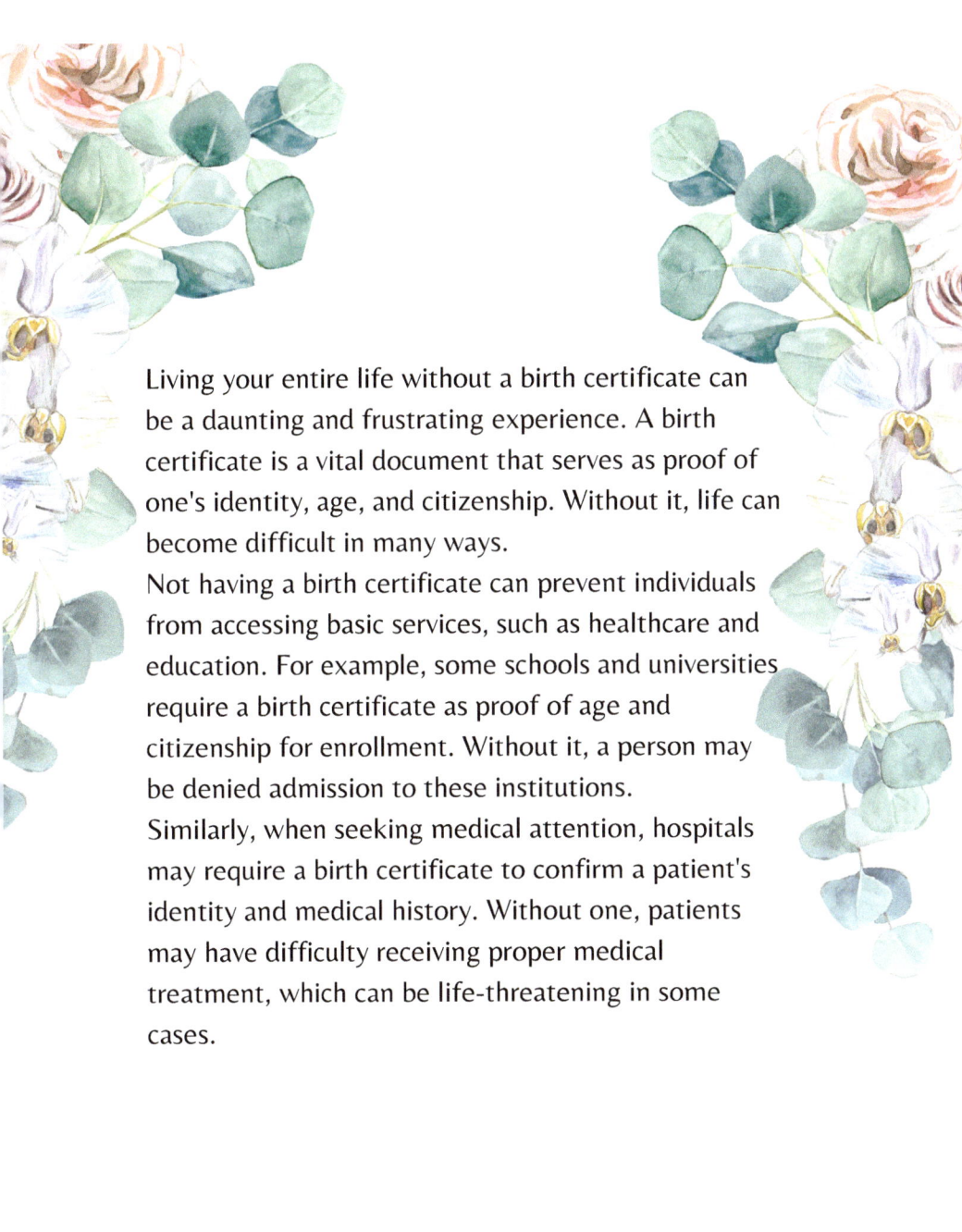

Living your entire life without a birth certificate can be a daunting and frustrating experience. A birth certificate is a vital document that serves as proof of one's identity, age, and citizenship. Without it, life can become difficult in many ways.

Not having a birth certificate can prevent individuals from accessing basic services, such as healthcare and education. For example, some schools and universities require a birth certificate as proof of age and citizenship for enrollment. Without it, a person may be denied admission to these institutions.

Similarly, when seeking medical attention, hospitals may require a birth certificate to confirm a patient's identity and medical history. Without one, patients may have difficulty receiving proper medical treatment, which can be life-threatening in some cases.

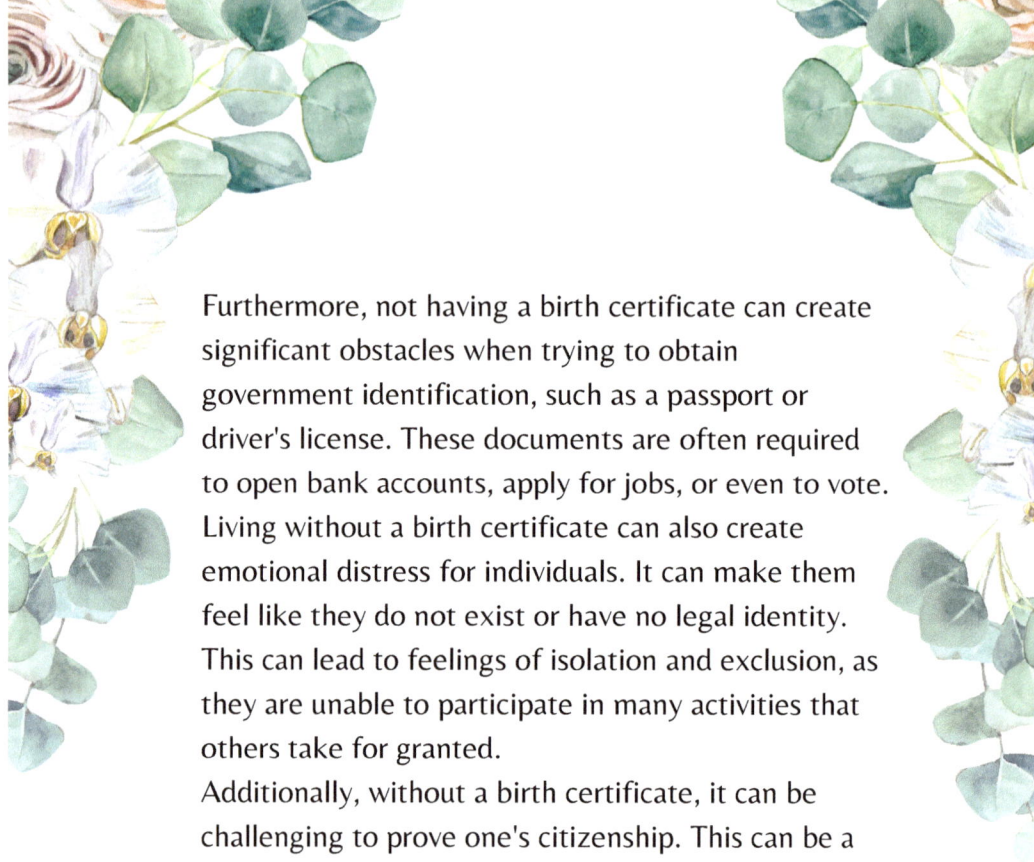

Furthermore, not having a birth certificate can create significant obstacles when trying to obtain government identification, such as a passport or driver's license. These documents are often required to open bank accounts, apply for jobs, or even to vote. Living without a birth certificate can also create emotional distress for individuals. It can make them feel like they do not exist or have no legal identity. This can lead to feelings of isolation and exclusion, as they are unable to participate in many activities that others take for granted.

Additionally, without a birth certificate, it can be challenging to prove one's citizenship. This can be a significant issue for those who were born in a foreign country or are descendants of immigrants. They may be at risk of being deported or denied basic rights as citizens.

In conclusion, living one's entire life without a birth certificate is a challenging and frustrating experience. It can hinder access to basic services, create emotional distress, and prevent individuals from obtaining legal identification and citizenship. It is essential that everyone has access to a birth certificate, as it is a fundamental document that provides proof of identity and citizenship. This is what my mother had to endure, we tried
countless times to obtain her birth certificate, they did not record it in Tulare, County, Ca. 1928
Mother I have created a birth certificate for you.

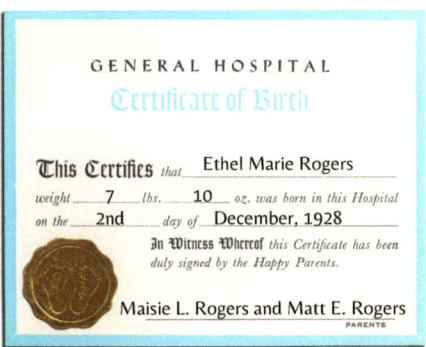

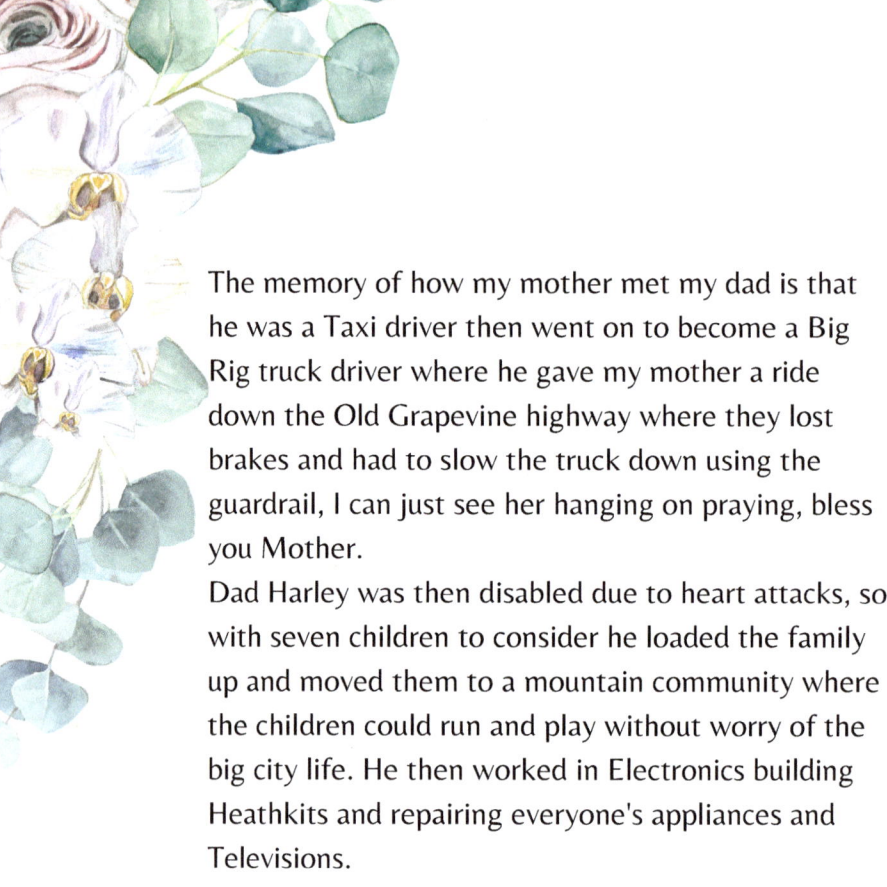

The memory of how my mother met my dad is that he was a Taxi driver then went on to become a Big Rig truck driver where he gave my mother a ride down the Old Grapevine highway where they lost brakes and had to slow the truck down using the guardrail, I can just see her hanging on praying, bless you Mother.

Dad Harley was then disabled due to heart attacks, so with seven children to consider he loaded the family up and moved them to a mountain community where the children could run and play without worry of the big city life. He then worked in Electronics building Heathkits and repairing everyone's appliances and Televisions.

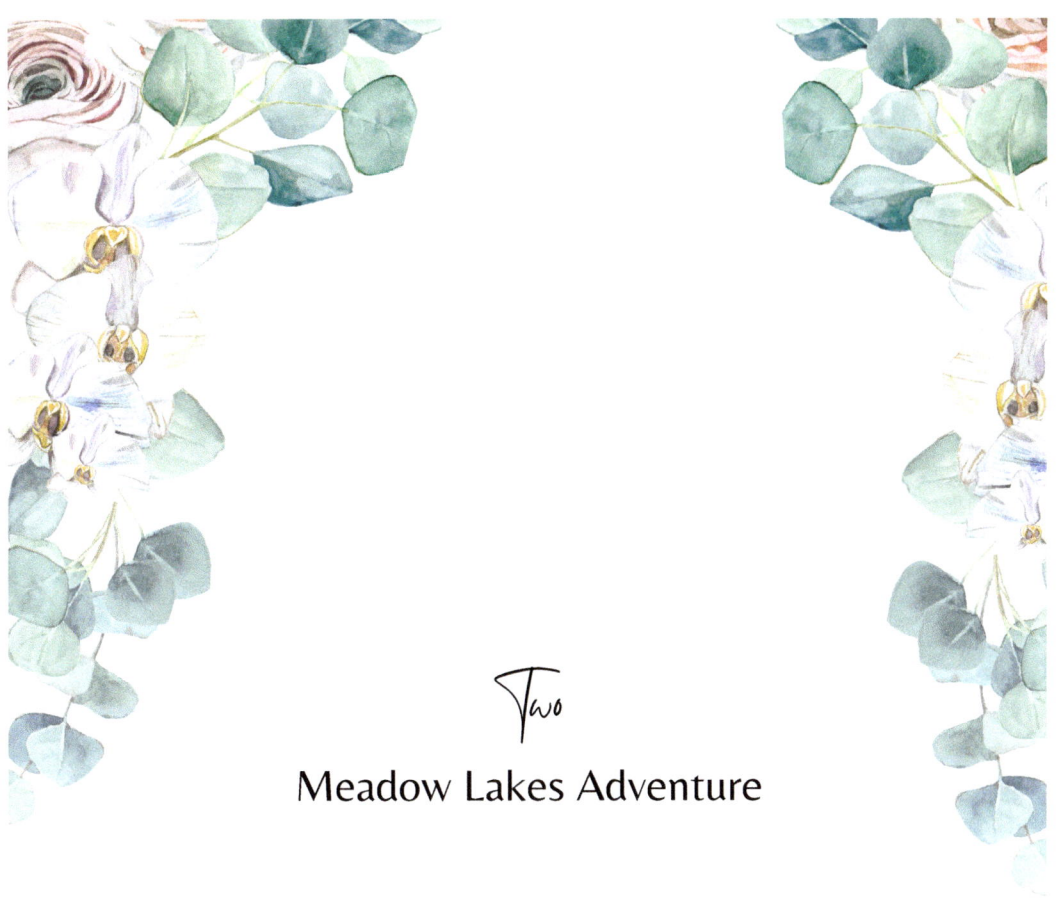

Two
Meadow Lakes Adventure

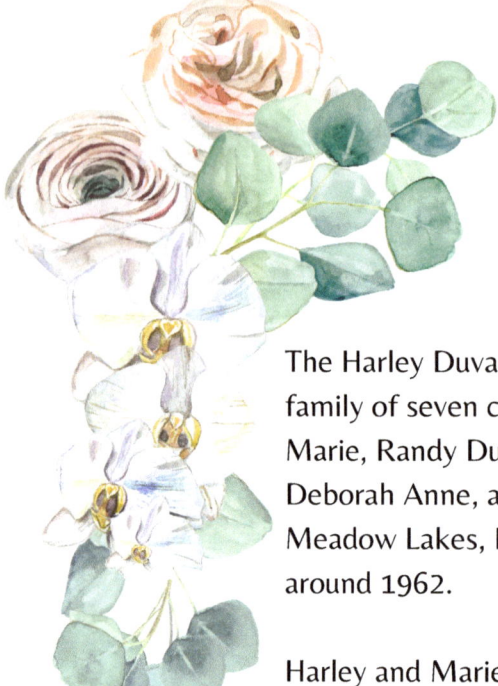
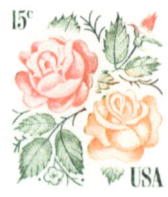

The Harley Duval and Ethel "Marie" Scott family of seven children, Danny Eugene, Linda Marie, Randy Duval, Ronald Lee, Terry Wayne, Deborah Anne, and Jeanette Lea, moved to Meadow Lakes, Fresno County, California around 1962.

Harley and Marie realized that raising this many children needed lots of fresh air and the great outdoors, if for their sanity alone. This is exactly what the tall pines and fresh air of Meadow Lakes offered.

All children attended the local schools of Pine Ridge, Auberry Union Elementary and Sierra Joint Union High School. On Sundays their parents would pack them into the car and take them to Church, or dad Harley would give them a little sermon in the living room, next to the fireplace.

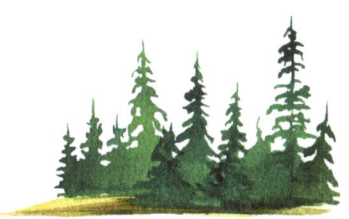

As the children grew, they found themselves treading through the snow to the bus stop and yes about a mile, but they could not be happier in this wonderful mountain playground. Sledding, swimming, fishing, and hiking were just a few of the favorite things to do.

Danny would graduate from Sierra High School and find himself landing a job in Fresno working for Fruehauf for 27 years, and raising a family of three children. He has grandchildren too.

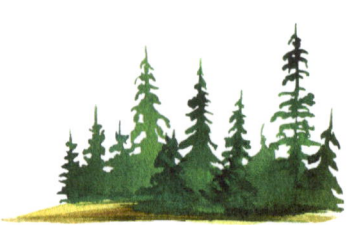

Linda prior to graduating entertained us all with a live television performance of Nancy Sinatra's "These Boots Are Made for Walking" I remember that day well, we had to wake up at the crack of dawn and with our little black and white tv, with barely any reception (we were at about 4500 ft elevation) but it came in clear, that day, Linda amazed us what a star. She had a job at Meadow Lakes working for local resident Dorothy Devine, what a great woman and character was Dorothy, Linda would entertain us with her stories of Dorothy and her work. Linda married and moved to Fresno, where she began her job working with special needs children, where she worked over 25 years. Linda has children and grandchildren.

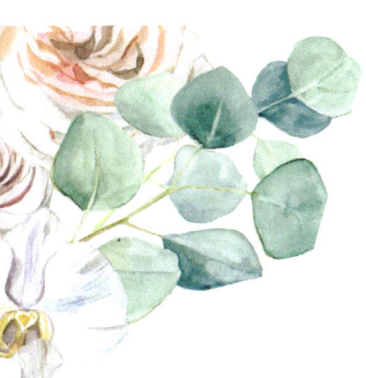

Randy, Ronnie and Terry all enlisted in the Army and left Meadow Lakes for the Viet Nam war. Ronnie was a medic-vac and re-upped countless times. He has children...he passed away from stroke, few years after he was honorably discharged.

Mother, Danny, Randy, Terry, Deborah, Jeanette were the artists. Jeanette loved pottery.

Randy had a painting sent to New York for a show, it was using wax and acrylic paint mediums. That was the same year Randy was Senior class president at Sierra High School.

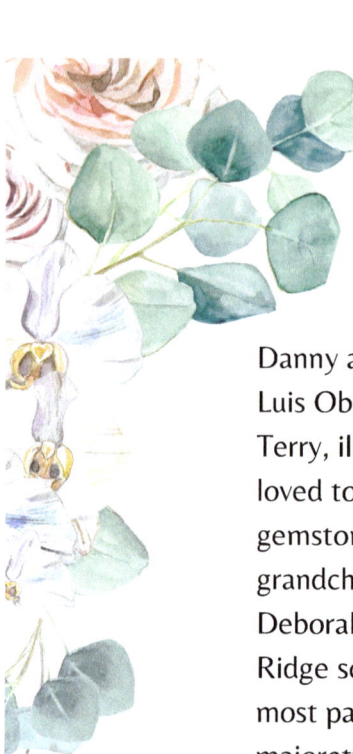

Danny and Mother, still placing art around San Luis Obispo, County, Ca.

Terry, illustrates beautiful drawings. He also loved to prospect and look for gold and gemstones, he has a beautiful daughter and grandchildren.

Deborah started marching in parades at Pine Ridge school in second grade and marched in most parades in elementary school, she was a majorette, pep girl and Drill Team, Linda too was on Drill Team. Deborah worked at Foothill Middle School in Prather, below Meadow Lakes, as paraprofessional, she directed the drama class - a class of 30, she retired early due to MS. Then went on to become a copyrighted jewelry designer and creator.

Jeanette, the littlest one followed the footsteps of her brother Ronnie and studied medicine, earning her credentials to become a certified nurse, having children and grandchildren of her own. Resides in Tennessee.

Harley passed away in 1979 leaving Marie with her children-she then found her love of art.

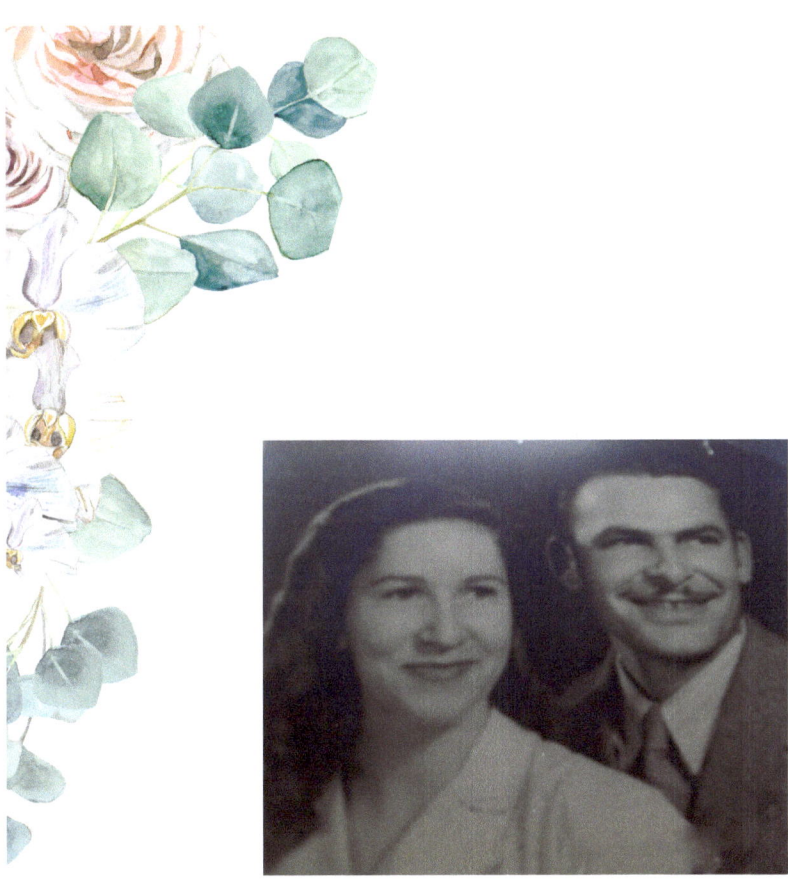

E.Marie and Harley D. Scott

One of the defining moments in her artistic journey was the 9/11 terrorist attacks on the Twin Towers in New York City. My Mother was deeply moved by the tragedy, and she felt compelled to create a painting that captured the emotional impact of the event. She spent weeks working on the painting, using bold colors and expressive brushstrokes to convey the sense of loss and sadness that she felt. The painting was a turning point for her, and it helped her gain recognition as an artist. They placed her art in an exhibit for the Veterans.

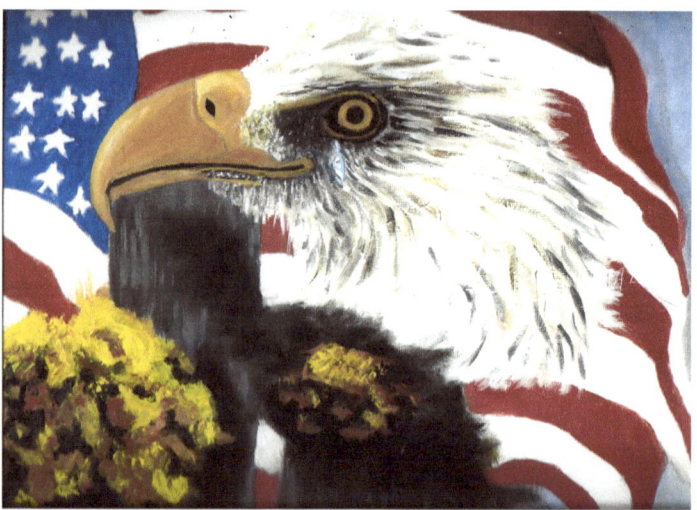

2001 Mother was 73 years old when she painted this. Twin Towers

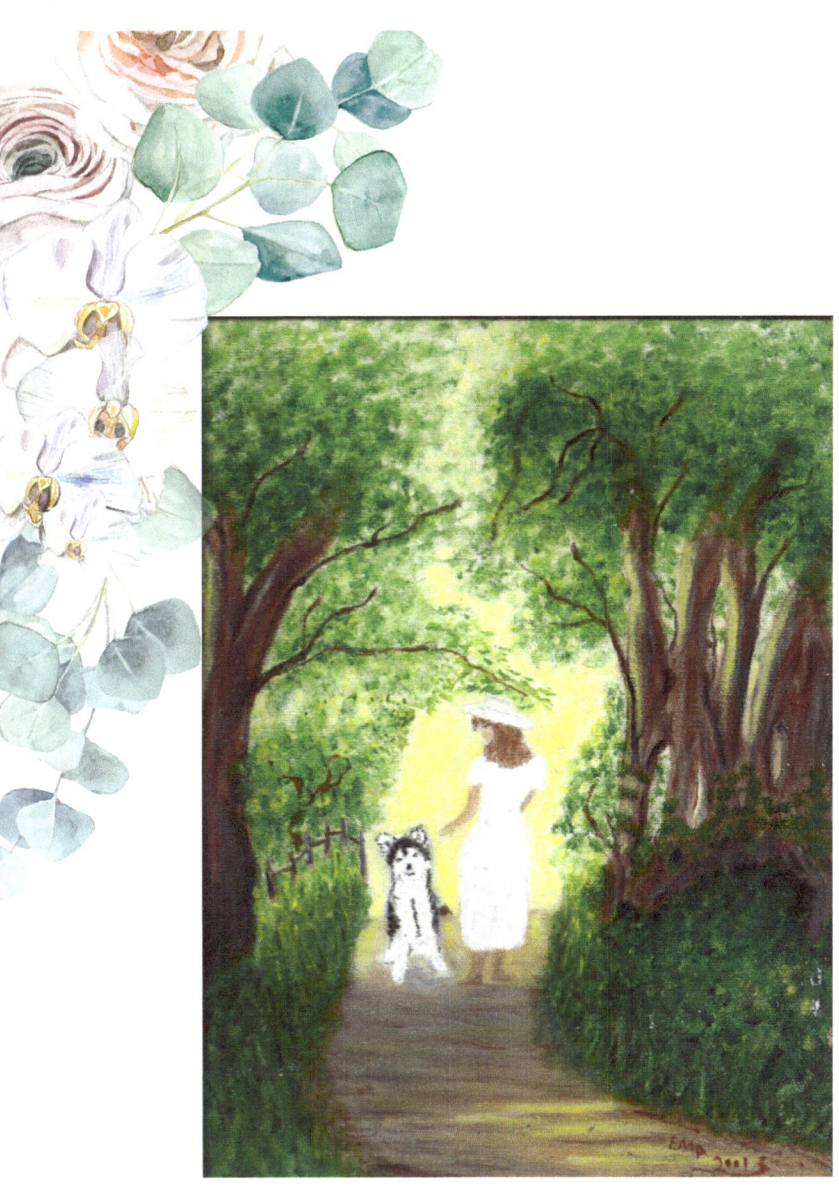

This is me and my dog Zephyr - 2001 Mother was 73 years old when she painted this. The dirt driveway to my gate.

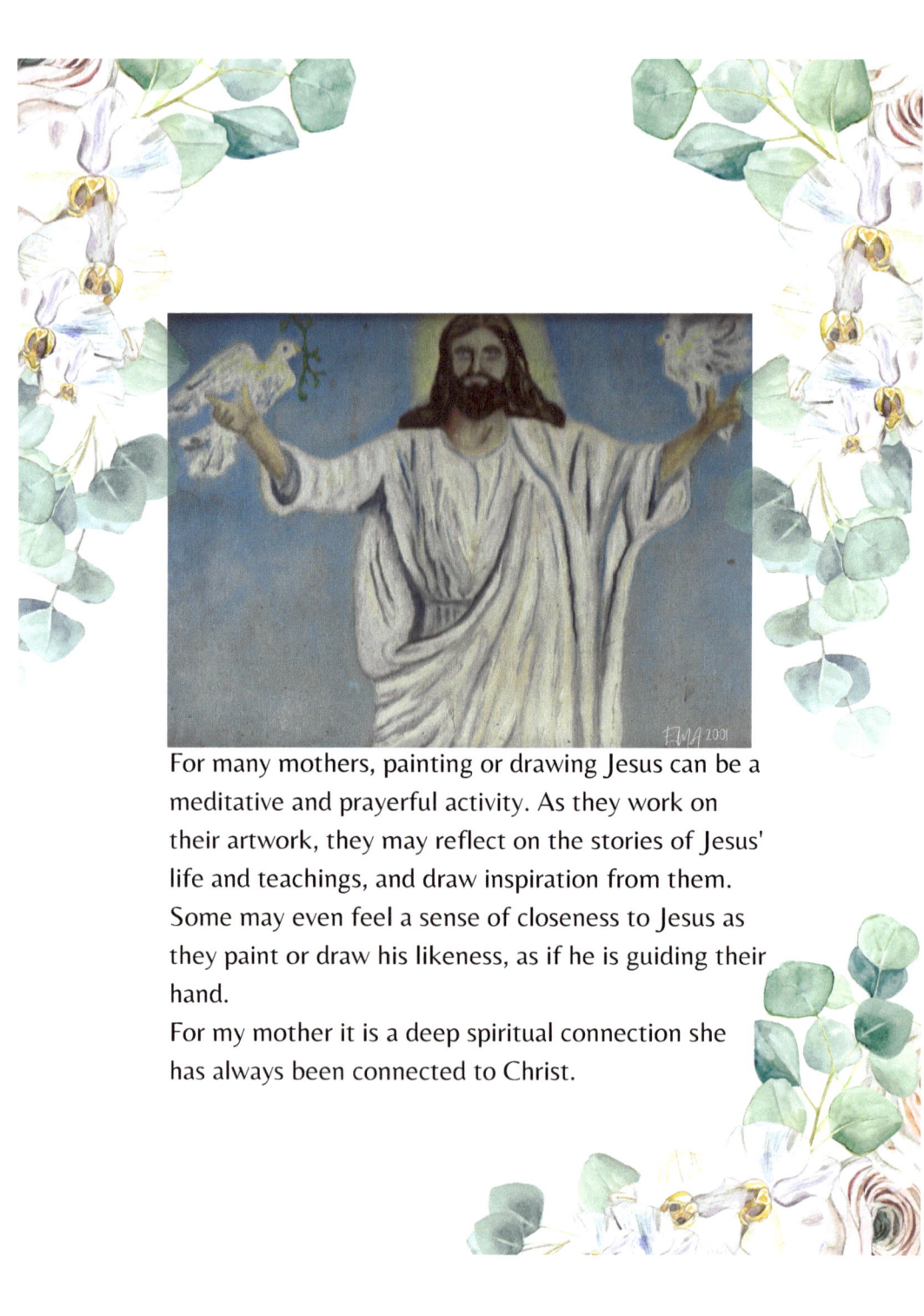

For many mothers, painting or drawing Jesus can be a meditative and prayerful activity. As they work on their artwork, they may reflect on the stories of Jesus' life and teachings, and draw inspiration from them. Some may even feel a sense of closeness to Jesus as they paint or draw his likeness, as if he is guiding their hand.

For my mother it is a deep spiritual connection she has always been connected to Christ.

Memories

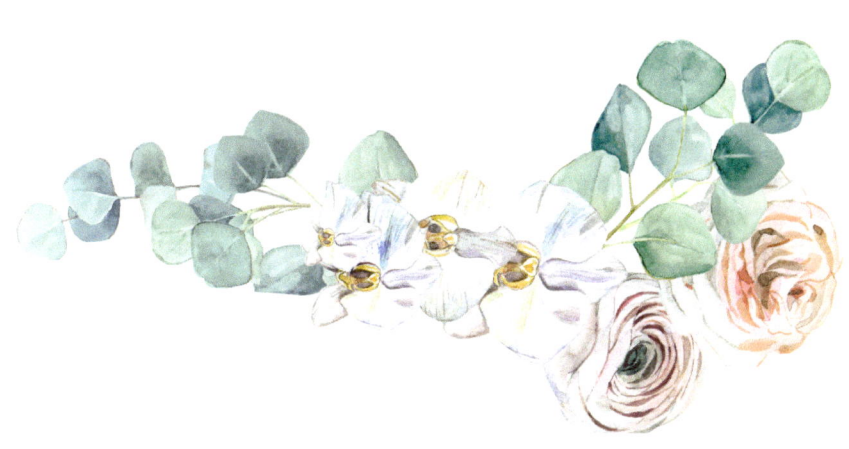

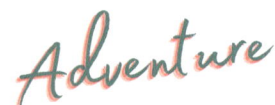

Adventure

Queen for a Day was an American radio and television game show that helped to usher in American listeners' and viewers' fascination with big-prize giveaway shows. Queen for a Day originated on the Mutual Radio Network on April 30, 1945, in New York City before moving to Los Angeles a few months later and ran until 1957. The show then ran on NBC Television from 1956 to 1960 and on ABC Television from 1960 to 1964.

The show became popular enough that NBC increased its running time from 30 to 45 minutes to sell more commercials, at a then-premium rate of $4,000 per minute.

A memory of my mother having a love of watching the show Queen for a Day, decided to one day, leave the
kids with dad and granddad and head to Hollywood on a Greyhounds bus, getting a room for the night and trying out for the show. She says she did not make it on the show but had a great adventure on her own.

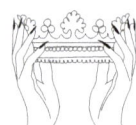

You were always a Queen to me Mother...

Driving

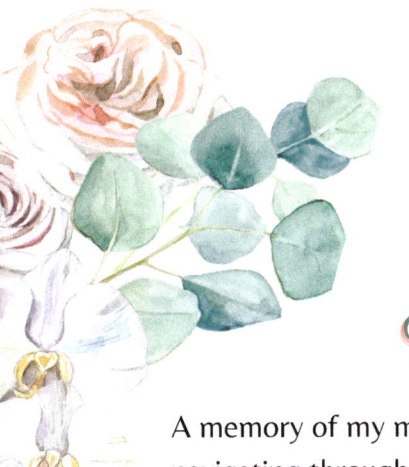

A memory of my mother learning to drive and navigating through challenging situations is a testament to the strength and perseverance of the human spirit, and a reminder of the importance of having a support system in our lives. I can still see Dad Harley standing in the driveway as my mother nervously backed the car out of the driveway it was downhill and a tree came close as she backed up, but we made it. A few years later my mother driving us all to town when a car crossed the center divider and Mother swerved and came close to hitting a telephone pole but again, we made it. I also remember a time when brother Terry was broken down in his car and in the middle of the night my mother got a tow bar and went to help, alone as Father was ill, again she made it.

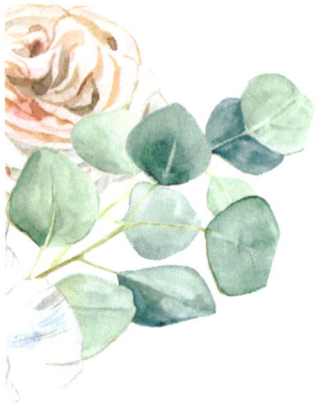

Another time in the car my mother thought it really funny while at a stop light to rev the engine because the guy in the car next to us was young and cute, he looked over at me and just smiled. One time we had a late-night school event and driving home it was dense fog, Mother did fine and we were almost to our turn off and we missed it going a mile or two when Mother realized "Oh! we missed our turn!" We had to drive back through the thick fog but we finally made it home. My Mother knew how to drive, I don't think she ever got a ticket or an accident. She hung up her license at 93.

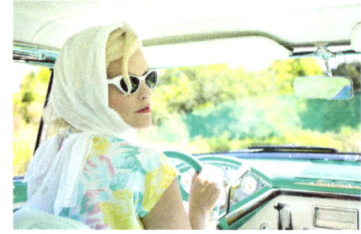

Image courtesy of canva.com

I have a memory of my mother's sacrifices for her children. One such memory that comes to mind is that of my mother who picked grapes so that I could have both a Majorette and Pep Girl outfit at school.

Being a Majorette or Pep Girl at school can be a dream come true for many young girls, but the uniforms and equipment required for these activities can be expensive, making it difficult for some families to afford them. In this instance, my mother recognized my passion for these activities and she worked tirelessly to ensure that I had the necessary outfits and equipment.

My mother spent long hours picking grapes in the fields, enduring the heat and hard labor to earn enough money to buy me the desired Majorette and Pep Girl outfits. Her hard work and dedication did not go unnoticed, and I was able to participate in both activities with pride and confidence, thank you Mother.

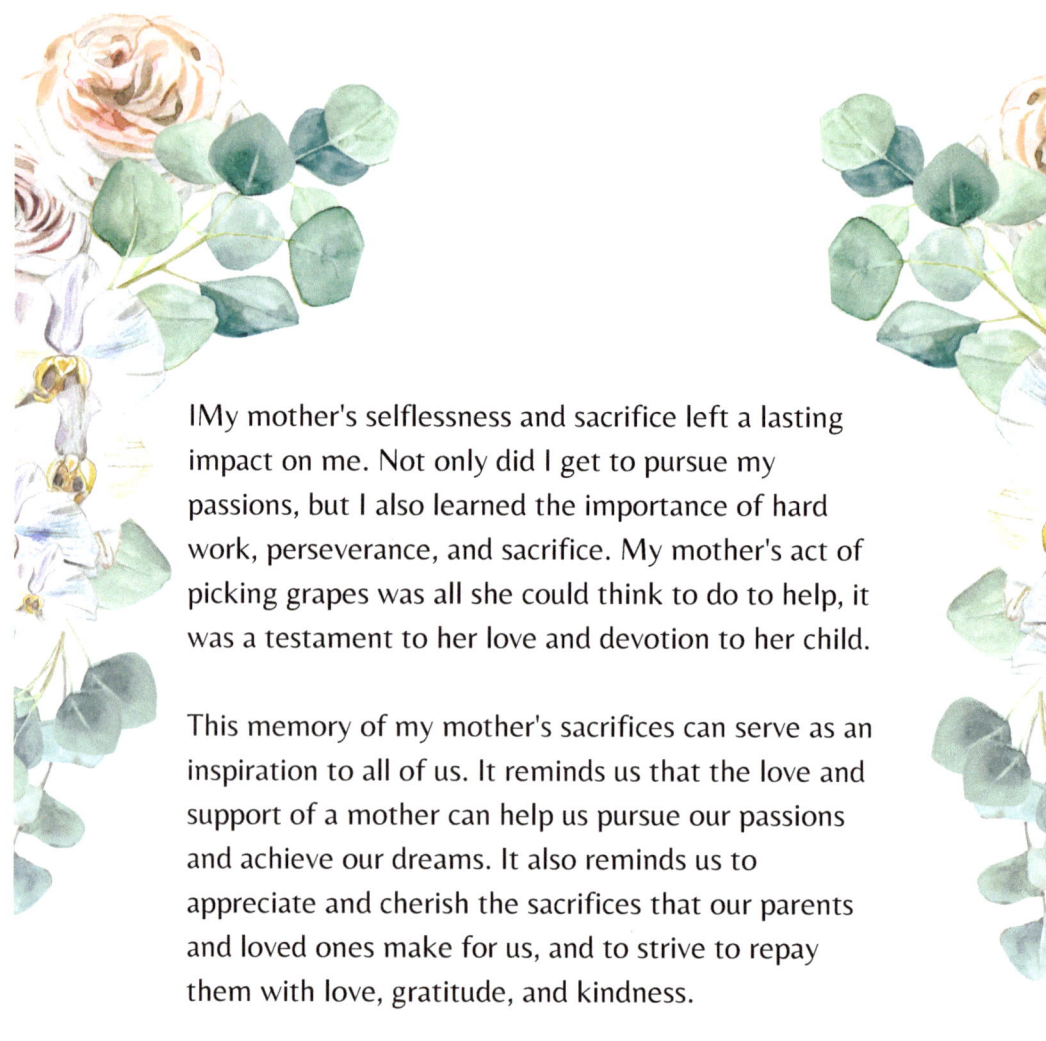

IMy mother's selflessness and sacrifice left a lasting impact on me. Not only did I get to pursue my passions, but I also learned the importance of hard work, perseverance, and sacrifice. My mother's act of picking grapes was all she could think to do to help, it was a testament to her love and devotion to her child.

This memory of my mother's sacrifices can serve as an inspiration to all of us. It reminds us that the love and support of a mother can help us pursue our passions and achieve our dreams. It also reminds us to appreciate and cherish the sacrifices that our parents and loved ones make for us, and to strive to repay them with love, gratitude, and kindness.

May 2023

Dearest Beloved Mother,

As I sit down to write this letter, my heart fills with so much love and gratitude for you. I turn 66 years old this month and wanted you to know, that you have been the constant in my life, the one person who has always been there for me no matter what. I am so blessed to have you as my mother.

From the moment I was born, you have been my rock. You held me close, nurtured me, and guided me through every step of my life. You were the one who taught me how to walk, how to talk, and how to be a good person. You were always there to wipe away my tears, to give me a hug when I needed it, and to celebrate my accomplishments with me.

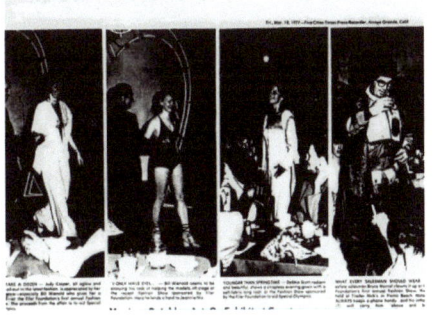

My Mother is wind beneath my wings...Deborah Models at Trader Nicks-Pismo Beach 1977

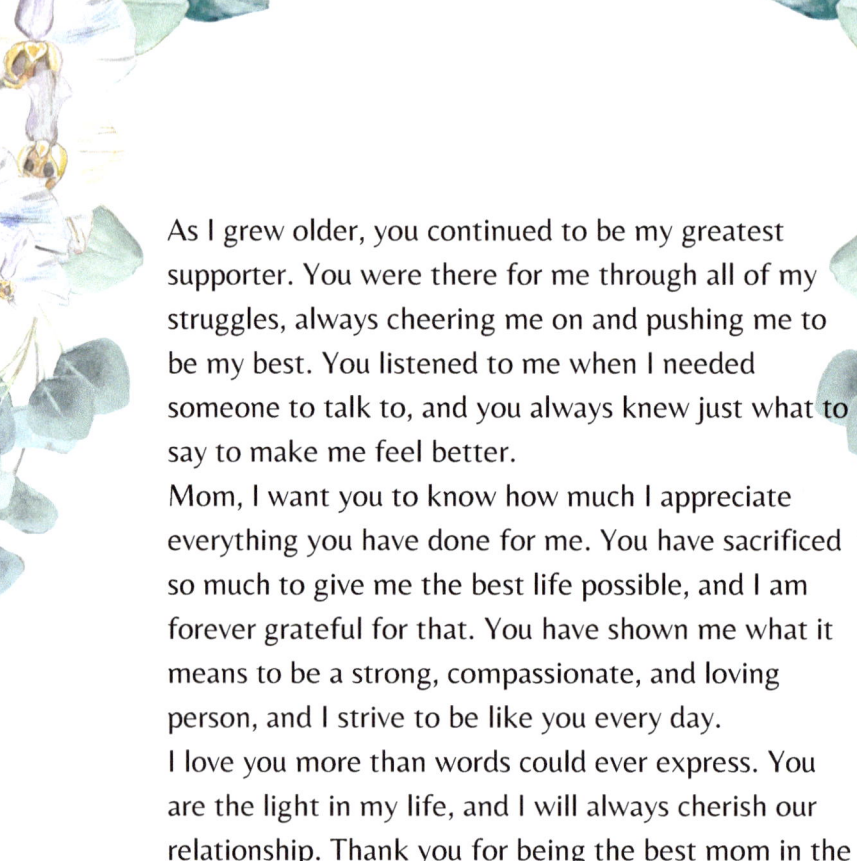

As I grew older, you continued to be my greatest supporter. You were there for me through all of my struggles, always cheering me on and pushing me to be my best. You listened to me when I needed someone to talk to, and you always knew just what to say to make me feel better.

Mom, I want you to know how much I appreciate everything you have done for me. You have sacrificed so much to give me the best life possible, and I am forever grateful for that. You have shown me what it means to be a strong, compassionate, and loving person, and I strive to be like you every day.

I love you more than words could ever express. You are the light in my life, and I will always cherish our relationship. Thank you for being the best mom in the world.

My forever and ever love,
Deborah Anne
2023

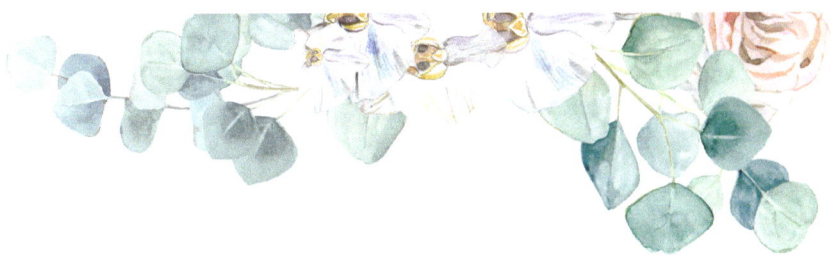

As the sun sets on her life, I am filled with both sadness and gratitude for the beautiful woman my mother is. Her love for art, animals, and children is unparalleled, and her selflessness and kindness touch the hearts of countless individuals. To many, she is a saint on earth.

Throughout her life, my mother's passion for art was a constant source of joy and inspiration. She has an eye for beauty and a talent for creating it, and her art captures the essence of the world around her in breathtaking ways. From the sweeping landscapes she painted, to her Jesus painting, her art is a testament to her boundless creativity and artistic vision.

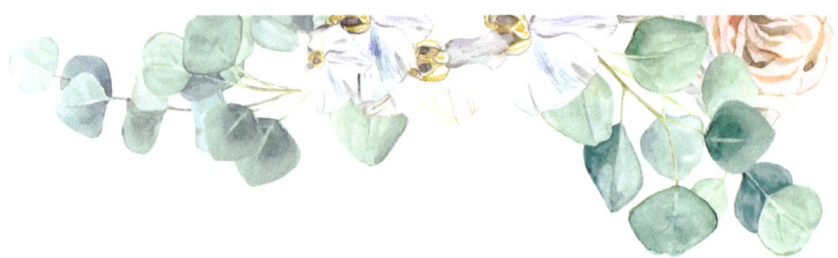

But it is not just her art that makes my mother special. Her love for animals is deep and abiding, and she has a way of connecting with creatures great and small that is truly remarkable. She has a particular fondness for dogs, and over the years she rescued and cared for countless strays, giving them love and a home.

And then there are the children. My mother has a gift for nurturing young minds and souls, and her warmth and compassion make her a beloved figure to her children, grandchildren and great grandchildren. My mother brings joy and love to every child she encounters.

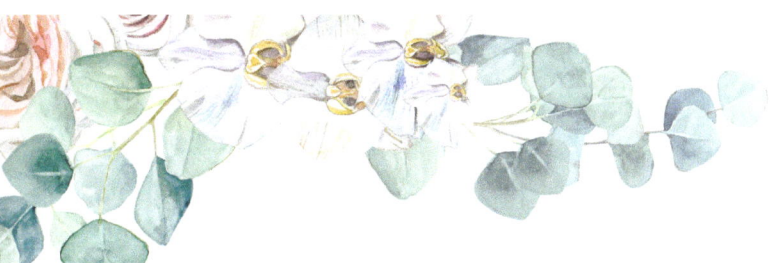

As my mother's life draws to a close, I am comforted by the knowledge that her legacy will live on. Her art will continue to inspire and delight, her love for animals will be remembered by those whose lives she touched, and her kindness and compassion will be a guiding light for generations to come.

To me, my mother is not just a saint, but a hero. She shows me what it means to live a life filled with purpose, passion, and love. I know that she will always be with me, in my memories, in my heart, and in the beauty of the world she helps create. I adore you Mother Ethel Marie Rogers-Scott-Andrews, thank you for my life and blessing me with your sweetness.

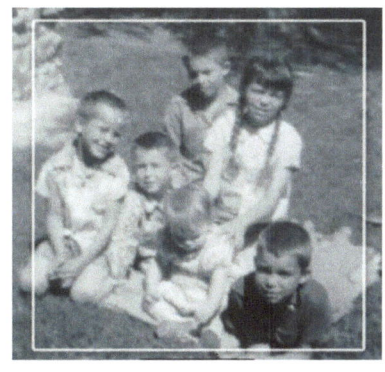

Scott children Jeanette was born two years later

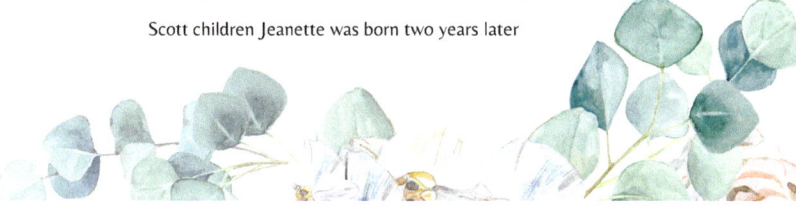

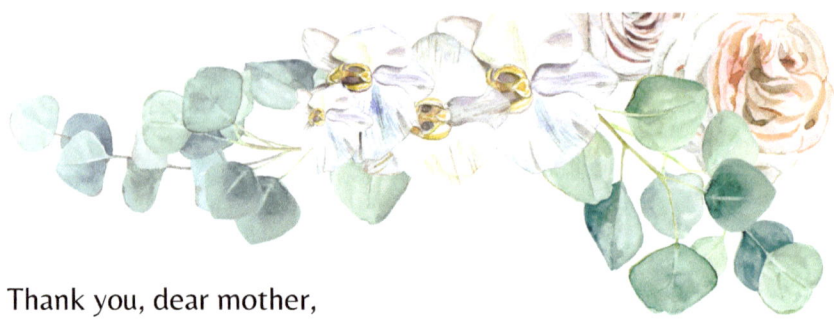

Thank you, dear mother,
For all that you do.   Your love and support   Carry me through.

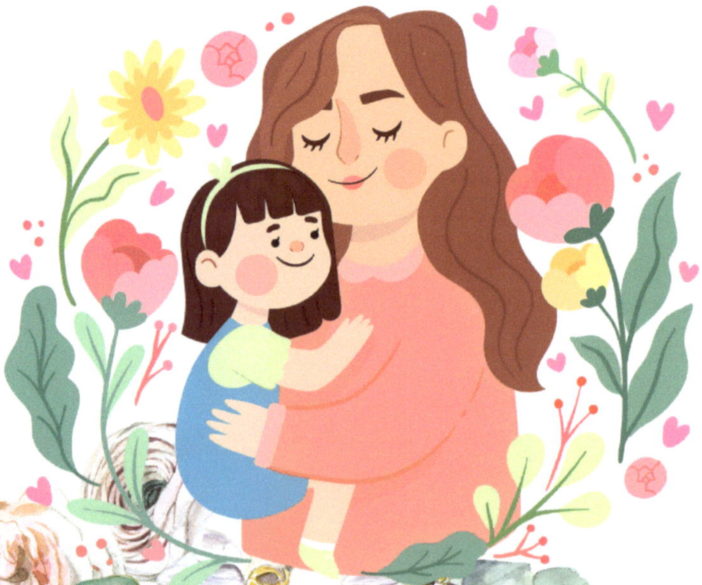

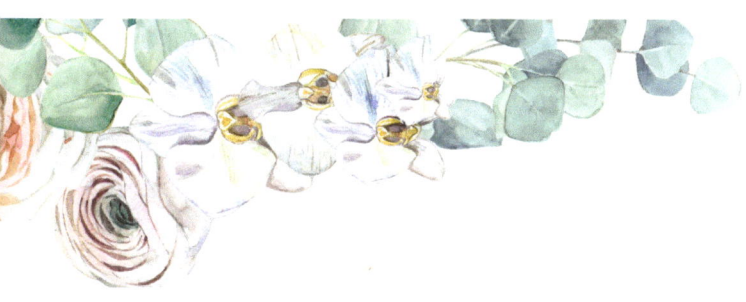

Thank you, dear mother,
For blessing me with brothers and sisters, nieces, nephews, great nieces and great nephews. So many blessings.

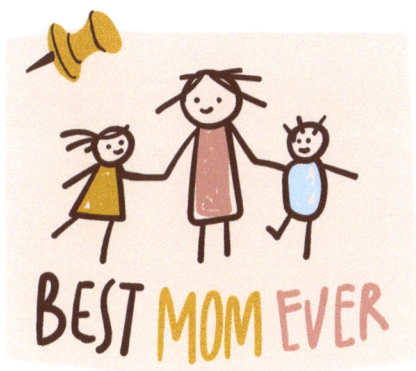

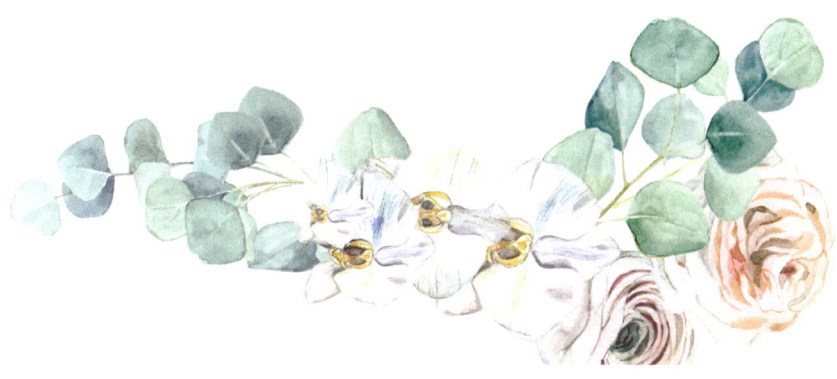

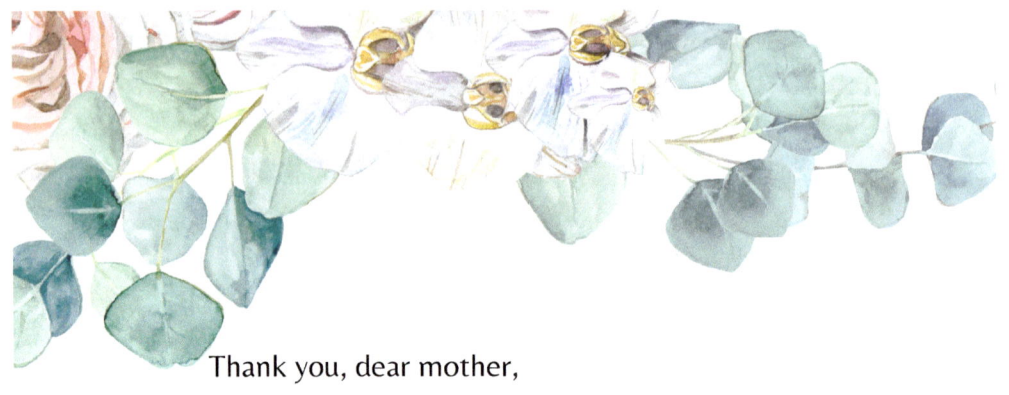

Thank you, dear mother,
For giving me life.

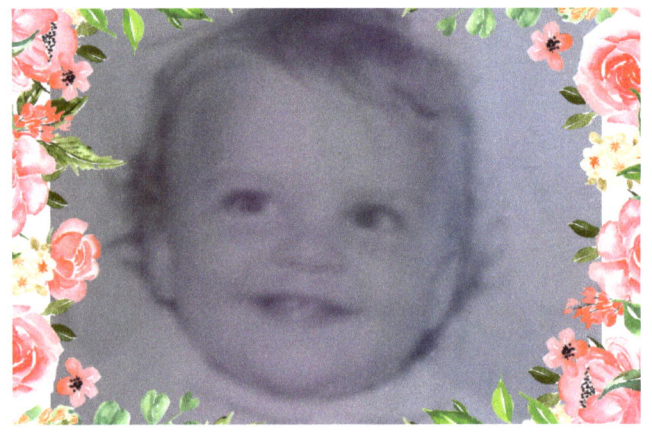

Deborah Anne Scott 1957

love you
Mom

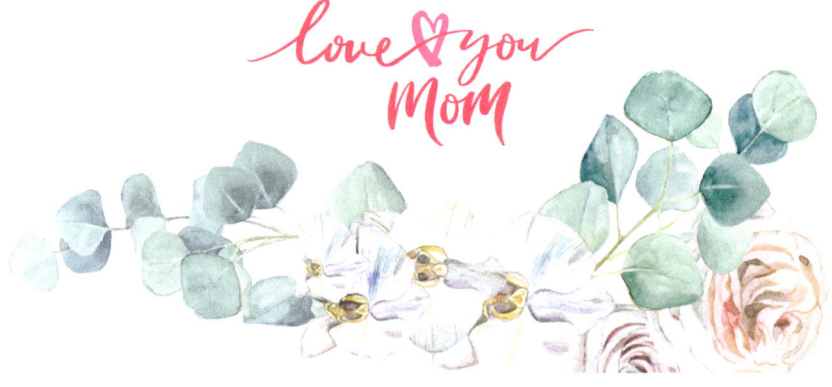

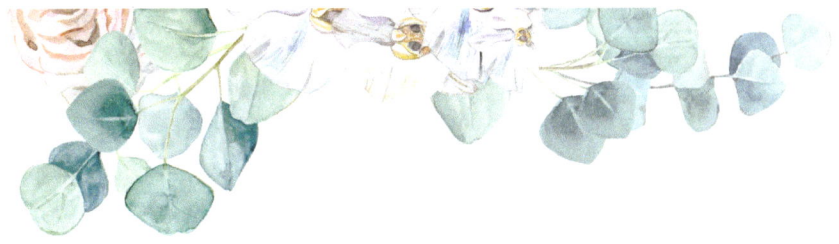

This book is dedicated to my dear family.

I wanted to take a moment to express my love and appreciation for each and every one of you, especially my dear mother.
Mom, you have always been my rock and my guiding light. Your unwavering love and support have helped me through the toughest of times. I am so grateful for all that you do for our family, and I know that I wouldn't be where I am today without you.

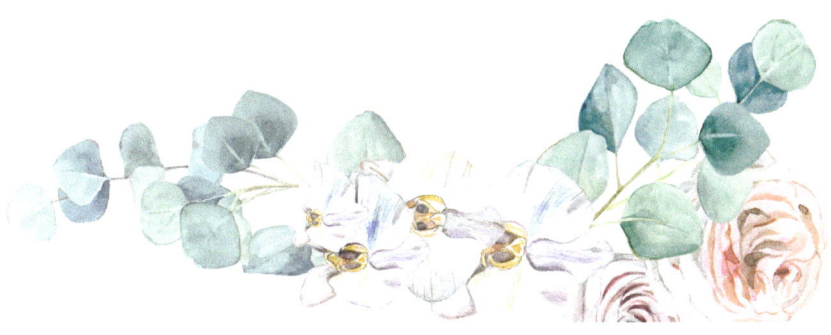

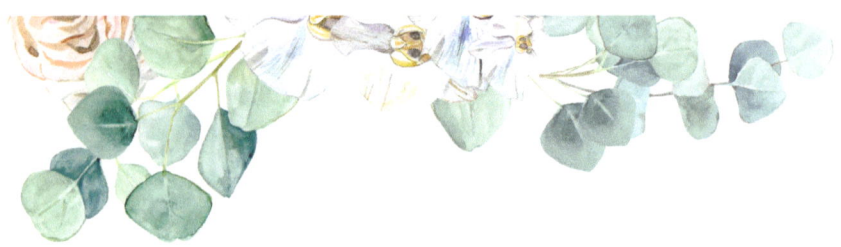

To my siblings, you all bring so much joy and laughter to my life. I cherish the memories we've made together and look forward to creating many more in the years to come.

Dad, your strength and wisdom were always an inspiration to me. Thank you for always being there for us and for being the backbone of our family as best as you could.

I love you all more than words can express.
Thank you for being my family.

Deborah

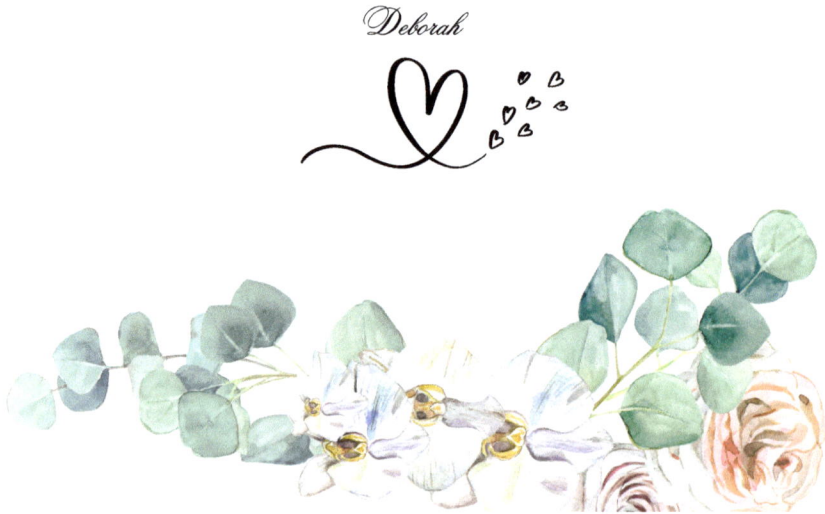

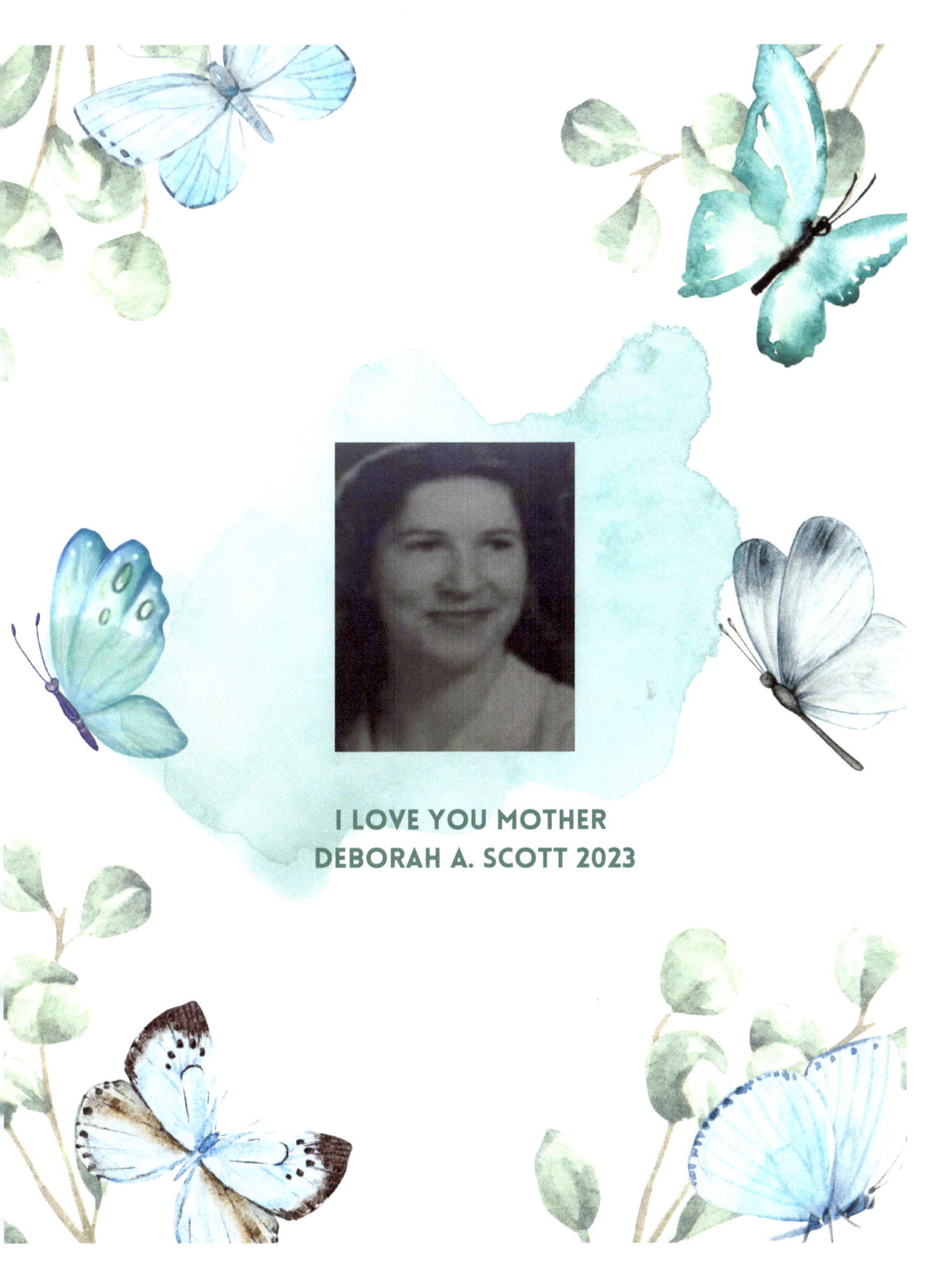

www.ingramcontent.com/pod-product-compliance
Lightning Source LLC
Chambersburg PA
CBHW040342220526
45473CB00009B/2762